Battle of the Beets

The Fight for Urban Farming Space

Table of Contents

Chapter 1. Introduction

Dive into the thriving world of urban agriculture with this vibrant Special Report: 'Battle of the Beets: The Fight for Urban Farming Space.' Watch as city streets transform into lush landscapes, and parking lots bloom into bountiful gardens. Discover the tenacity and innovation of urban farmers fighting for ground in the concrete jungle, where every rooftop and balcony becomes a battlefield. In this riveting exploration, we'll unravel the challenges, victories, and unexpected relationships formed, all with a shared goal of producing fresh, local food. Get ready to root for these modern-day, green-thumbed warriors as they redefine what it means to farm. After reading this paragraph, one thing should be clear: this is a tale you wouldn't want to miss! Ready to dig in? Secure your copy of the 'Battle of the Beets' special report today!

Chapter 2. The Rise of Concrete Jungles

The transformation of urban spaces from concrete jungles into flourishing farming entities is a story, unlike any of its kind. The heroes? An army not of suits and ties, but of shovels and seeds. The landscape? A battleground of asphalt and steel, not fields and pastures. This narrative unravels the rise of urban farms amidst the backdrop of concrete jungles.

2.1. The Cries of the Concrete

Our tale starts in the late 20th century with growing urban population and an increasing disconnect between people and their source of food. Cities were filled with hustle and bustle, creating a fast-paced, often stressful, lifestyle. The eye-catching skyscrapers and infinite paved ways painted a picture of development but hid a sad truth – we, the humans, were losing touch with Mother Nature. Streets that once saw the fall of leaves were replaced with highways that echoed with honks. Remarkably, there was a rising group of heroes who saw potential within the reaches of these concrete landscapes.

2.2. Sowing Seeds Amidst Steel

These daring urban pioneers, armed with a desire to reestablish connection with the essence of life, spotted unlikely allies in the sprawls of steel and concrete. They dreamt of an urban landscape brimming not only with architectural marvels but teeming with life brought forth from the ground. They saw rooftops, vacant spaces, parking lots, even balconies of apartments as potential mini-farms. The notion was simple yet revolutionary: Convert available urban spaces into productive farming landscapes. And thus, the urban farming wave began.

Seeds were sown, watered, and nurtured in containers and elevated beds, atop roofs, and within desolate lots. The aim was not to create commercial farming entities, rather establish a network of sustainable, localized food production initiatives.

2.3. Sprouting Success Stories

The pioneers of urban farming fought tooth and nail against the logistics and bureaucratic convolution that often plague innovations in urban planning. But, the results were well worth the struggle. Vacant, often derelict, urban spaces were now filled with lush greenery, bringing not only visual charm but also a sense of peace and tranquility amidst the chaos of urban living.

These initiatives were not just about cultivating crops; they were also about cultivating communities. Spontaneous relationships flourished as more and more city-dwellers started to appreciate the humble satisfaction of pulling out a veggie grown in their apartment balcony or the community garden around the corner. The concrete jungle started teeming with not just vegetables and herbs, but stories of resilience, cooperation, and rediscovered connections.

2.4. Of Challenges and Triumphs

Urban farming was not, and is still not, without its challenges. Urban space is a prized commodity. Land availability and cost are significant barriers, as are logistical constraints. Yet the urban farming heroes navigated the complexities of the urban ecosystem with passion and ingenuity, tackling zoning laws, pollution, and limited spaces with thoughtful strategies and even technology.

Despite the grueling challenges, the victories are worth celebrating. Cities worldwide have witnessed the transformation of derelict public spaces into vibrant community farms, rooftops of commercial buildings turning into lush gardens yielding the freshest of produce, and front yards of homes becoming the source of the next meal. The transformation has also catalyzed environmental benefits, including better air quality and reduced heat islands at the heart of our concrete jungles.

2.5. Sustainable Cities: Our Shared Future

Given our current climate crisis, our urban farming heroes find themselves as the avant-gardists of a movement more significant than themselves—the pursuit of sustainability. The lessons from the rise of urban farming in the concrete jungles are more relevant now than ever. The narrative of turning concrete and steel into green, productive landscapes is a testament to the power of sustainability.

As we build the future of our cities, this urban farming chapter must be taken into account. We are not just city-dwellers; we are stewards of our shared urban landscapes. Let's not just pave our cities with concrete and erect buildings of steel. Let's paint them green, grow food, cultivate relationships, fight climate change, and build sustainable cities that breathe. The rise of the concrete jungle may seem an unlikely saga, but it's one that heralds hope for not just our cities, but our planet.

This first chapter of 'Battle of the Beets' special report ends here. The urban agricultural revolution has just begun, the thrilling journey awaits in the forthcoming chapters. As we progress, the concrete jungles' transformation starts to unfurl, showcasing the unwavering dedication and strategic struggle of our modern, green-thumbed warriors.

Chapter 3. Seeds of Change: The Origin of Urban Farming

Stepping onto the asphalt, one wouldn't typically imagine the urban landscape as fertile ground for agriculture. Yet, this is precisely the origin of urban farming and its counterintuitive nature is part of its charm. As today's urban farmers sow seeds of change, they are merely treading a path established centuries ago. In fact, the concept of urban farming is not a recent phenomenon. Thousands of years ago, farming wasn't the domain of the outskirts of the city, but was deeply interwoven into the urban framework itself.

3.1. Urban Agriculture in Ancient Times

The domestication of plants and animals signified the dawn of agriculture approximately 10,000 years ago, dating back to the Neolithic period. However, agriculture practiced within city limits has been traced back to ancient civilizations across the globe. In Central America, the Aztecs constructed 'chinampas' - man-made islands teeming with vegetation in the middle of lakes and canals. This innovative solution enabled them to cultivate crops year-round, regardless of changing seasons or weather patterns. Similarly, in ancient Egypt, civilization flourished along the Nile River's fertile banks, integrating agriculture into everyday urban life.

3.2. From Need to Hobby

As civilizations evolved, agricultural practices became confined to rural areas, owing to industrialization and the growth of cities. Urban areas focused on commerce, industries, and services while rural regions were tasked with providing them with food supplies.

Yet, times of crisis often led to the resurgence of urban farming. During both World Wars, 'Victory Gardens' sprang up in Britain and the United States, where community members were encouraged to utilize all available space - gardens, rooftops, and vacant plots - to grow food and help sustain the population during food shortages.

Post World War II, urban farming mostly shrunk into a hobbyist's pursuit until the 1970s oil, economic, and environmental crises ignited a new interest in self-sustainability. This sparked movements advocating for community gardens and local farming, particularly in the United States and Europe.

3.3. The Advent of Modern Urban Farming

The start of the 21st century brought about a significant shift in urban farming dynamics. The focus ceases to be solely about survival or self-sustainability. It began incorporating ecological concerns, food security, and community development. The digital revolution further bolstered this shift, equipping urban farmers with innovative tools and techniques to maximize outputs in confined spaces.

Community-supported agriculture (CSA) programs, rooftop gardens, and vertical farming started gaining momentum, all indicating towards a new age of urban farming. Innovative farms like Brooklyn Grange, one of the world's largest rooftop soil farms, are revolutionizing the perception of farming within city confines.

3.4. The Urban Agriculture Revolution Today

Today, urban farming manifests itself in various forms ranging from small-scale kitchen gardens to large-scale rooftop farms spanning acres. Urban farmers curate symbiotic environments, optimizing the coexistence of various species and transforming mundane cityscape into a lush, edible oasis. Often, these spaces transcend food production and become hubs for community events, ecological education, and relaxation.

People feel more and more connected to their food and empowered by the possibility of producing it themselves. Millennials and young adults, in particular, are leading this revolution. They are increasingly realizing the critical role of local, organic food in maintaining physical health and environmental sustainability.

Overall, the rise of urban farming today symbolizes humanity's resilience and adaptability, reflecting an ongoing transition towards sustainable living within urban landscapes. As our cities continue to stretch their boundaries, every balcony, rooftop, and vacant plot has the potential to turn into a fertile field, just as it did in ancient times.

In the next chapters, we will delve into the challenges faced by modern urban farmers and the creative solutions they are devising. But it's essential to remember that, despite the evolution in practices, technology, and motivations, the underlying premise of urban farming remains constant: the resilience of humankind to adapt and thrive, using all possible resources - even in the heart of concrete jungles.

Chapter 4. Microgreens in Microspaces: Utilizing Limited Terrain

Urban farming, in many ways, transcends typical notions of agriculture. It isn't confined to wide, open tracts of land. It is a mosaic composed of cleverly utilised spaces that are often overlooked. Microgreens are one of the cornerstones of urban agriculture. These tiny, nutrient-rich plants are adept at thriving even in cramped locations. This chapter is an exploration of the ways in which these tiny powerhouses are cultivated in urban spaces, defying restrictions, and their significance in the grand scheme of urban farming.

4.1. The Might of Microgreens

Microgreens, despite their diminutive stature, pack a mighty punch both nutritionally and agriculturally. Harvested within 7-14 days from when they're sown, these young vegetable greens are about 1-3 inches tall. Their nutrient content is, however, anything but tiny. Studies have revealed that microgreens possess up to 40 times more vital nutrients than their mature counterparts. This, compounded with their ability to grow in small spaces, makes them invaluable to urban farming.

Urban farmers find microgreens an attractive crop due to their short growth cycle, allowing for rapid turnover. Thanks to their size, they can be grown in a multitude of urban environments - from an inner-city balcony to a rooftop or even a kitchen counter.

4.2. The Garden in your Window

One innovative concept that has proven successful is window farming, where microgreens are planted in hanging containers affixed to windows. This model maximizes sunlight usage, essential for plant growth, without taking up ample horizontal space.

To start a window farm, one needs clear, plastic bottles that have been sanitized; a handful of microgreen seeds; growth medium (compost or hydroponic solution); and string to secure the setup. The bottles can be arranged in a vertical chain, with their bottoms cut out to facilitate water flow. Each bottle acts as a pot for the microgreens, and their transparency allows maximum light absorption.

4.3. Rooftop Dominions

For more adventurous urban farmers, the roof surface provides an extensive 'field' for microgreen cultivation. Rooftops are usually devoid of shade and obtain optimum sunlight throughout the day. One hindrance could be the need for a weight limit. Still, microgreens, with their shallow root system and lightweight growing medium, are a perfect fit.

Ways to start a rooftop microgreen garden range from low-tech (using multiple trays filled with growing medium) to high-tech (drip irrigation systems with climate and moisture sensors). Regardless of the approach, a fundamental understanding of the environmental conditions specific to one's rooftop (such as wind speed, sunlight exposure, and temperature variations) is crucial.

4.4. Turnkey Microgreens in Shipping Containers

The incredible evolution of urban farming introduces us to yet another wonder—the concept of farming inside shipping containers. These self-contained units are typically equipped with a hydroponic system, LED lights that mimic sunlight, climate control, and sometimes automated harvesting.

As microgreens require a controlled environment more than vast space, they have become the star crop of shipping container farming. These operations can be incredibly productive, with some farmers harvesting 50-100 pounds of microgreens weekly!

4.5. The Importance of Community in Microspaces

Despite the myriad methods of growing microgreens in small spaces, perhaps the most effective method is the simplest—growing in one's backyard, whether in soil or a simple hydroponic setup. The process becomes even more impactful when it develops into communal activity, promoting sustainable living and fostering stronger community bonds.

Communities can pool their resources, share knowledge, and even establish cooperative selling platforms. For instance, everyone in an apartment block could grow different types of microgreens, exchange their produce, or even sell in local farmer markets.

In conclusion, microgreens offer us a remarkable model of efficiency, richness, and resilience by thriving in various microspaces of urban settings. Through ingenious innovations, and the tenacity of our green thumbed urban farmers, these tiny greens are crossing new frontiers, adding a touch of verdancy in an otherwise concrete-dominated landscape. The promise that microgreens hold for urban farming is immense—a promise of sustenance, ecological balance, and community bonding. Their growth in the concrete jungle is not just a fight for space—it's a celebration of life.

Chapter 5. Aquaponics in Apartments: Innovations in Urban Agriculture

As part of the vanguard of urban agriculture innovation, coupling fish with plant production in aquaponics systems has taken urban farming to new heights—quite literally, as these systems have found their way into city apartment buildings. These types of farming systems are the future of food in our increasingly urbanized world, and this chapter will delve into the fascinating world of aquaponics in apartment living.

Aquaponics combines aquaculture (raising fish) with hydroponics (the soil-less growing of plants) in one integrated system. The water from the aquaculture part of the system circulates through a hydroponic system where the by-products from the fish are filtered out by the plants as vital nutrients, after which the cleansed water is recirculated back to the aquaculture system. This process creates a symbiotic relationship between the plants and the fish in the system.

5.1. Triumphant Trials and Triumphs: Experimentations in the Beginning

In the 1980s, interested parties began rigorous experimenting with aquaponics systems in the urban setting. Historically, the two separate systems of aquaculture and hydroponics posed unique challenges that seemed to cancel out the other. Traditional soil-less hydroponics required expensive nutrients to feed the plants and frequent water changes. Aquaculture, on the other hand, required the water to be removed and replaced continuously to remove the fish's excrements. However, scientists and experimenters discovered that these two problems solution lies within the other, giving rise to what we know today as aquaponics.

5.2. The Apartment Aquaponics Advantage

Aquaponics in apartments can provide significant advantages to urban dwellers. The primary advantage is that such systems don't rely on soil—an asset often limited in an urban environment—and utilize a closed-loop water system. Closed-loop systems are designed to reuse water, meaning they use up to 90% less water than traditional farming methods. Moreover, these systems also take considerably less space up compared to conventional farming, allowing for more food to be grown per square foot. It cannot be understated how crucial this is in an urban setting, where land is scarcer as compared to the countryside.

5.3. Hydroponic Heroes: The Architects of High-rise Gardens

Interest in aquaponics for apartment living is ballooning, giving rise to businesses and consultants offering solutions for creating these ecosystems in urban environments. One such hydroponic hero, Kate Zidar, has designed a rooftop aquaponics system in Brooklyn. With a graduate degree in environmental planning, Zidar understood the potential for aquaponics in urban food production and, with a group of volunteers, converted an unused rooftop into a lush food production site.

Zidar's success underscores the crucial fact of these apartment aquaponic systems: aside from their practicality and efficiency, there's beauty in growing your own food in such a unique way. The process can be educational, therapeutic, and, most importantly, empowering to urban dwellers who would otherwise not have access to grow their own fresh produce.

5.4. Balancing Act: The Changes in Climate and Control

Climate changes, yet another challenge around the corner for urban agriculture. Traditional soil-based farming can be adversely affected by unpredictable weather patterns. Consequently, the indoor, controlled nature of aquaponics presents a clear advantage. When properly managed, apartment aquaponic systems can remain relatively unaffected by external weather issues.

Yet, one must still consider the unique challenges posed by using aquaponics in an apartment setting. This includes the need to carefully balance the fish-to-plant ratio for optimal health and growth, maintaining the appropriate temperature conditions for fish and plants to thrive, and dealing with pest issues that can occur due to the indoor environment. Despite these challenges, a well-maintained aquaponics system can produce a consistent and significant yield of both produce and fish meat, providing a sustainable source of nutrition.

5.5. Closing Thoughts: The Future of Farming at Home

In conclusion, aquaponics in apartments presents a unique and exciting opportunity to redefine urban agriculture. Despite the potential challenges, urban dwellers who embark on the aquaponics journey discover a rewarding mix of sustainability, self-reliance, and interaction with nature, all without ever having to leave their apartment. It's clear that the future of farming in our cities may lie not just in empty lots or rooftops, but also within the walls of our high-rise apartment buildings.

Urban agriculture will undoubtedly continue to evolve, and aquaponics will play a significant role in its progress. This progress is the heart of our story—the Battle of the Beets—as this form of farming continues to go...upwards and onwards!

Chapter 6. Skyscraper Farms: A Look at Vertical Farming

The face of farming as we know it is being transformed. Picture a skyscraper, towering high above a city's skyline, where each floor is dedicated to rows of lush, thriving crops instead of sterile office cubicles. Welcome to the world of vertical farming - a concept that turns traditional agriculture on its side, embracing the idea of growing upwards rather than outwards.

6.1. The Genesis of Vertical Farming

The concept of vertical farming was pioneered by Dr. Dickson Despommier, a Professor of Environmental Health Sciences at Columbia University. Disappointed with the underwhelming results from traditional rooftop gardens, he recommended stacking them on top of one another inside the buildings. This revolutionary idea would lead to what we today recognize as vertical farming.

With vertical farming, crops are planted in stacked layers, typically in controlled indoor environments. These plants can be grown year-round, regardless of the weather conditions outside. Moreover, they require significantly less space, and use up to 70-95% less water than traditional farming, leading to a major breakthrough in sustainable agriculture.

6.2. Turning Skyscrapers into Farms

Modern vertical farms are a striking blend of nature and technology. While the specifics of their design vary, the basic principle is often the same - maximize space, control the environment, and optimize for efficiency.

Typically, vertical farms are structured around a central light source, usually a high-efficiency LED, which provides the necessary illumination for plant growth. Plants are lined up on shelving systems, receiving just the right balance of light and nutrients, while robots and sensors handle the bulk of the farm labor. This automated, precision agriculture allows vertical farms to run with minimal human intervention.

Venturing into a vertical farm, you'd encounter rows upon rows of leafy greens moving in synchrony along conveyor belts. They snake their way through the farm, each plant bathed in an unearthly purple light, the telltale sign of LED-lit chlorophyll absorption.

6.3. Necessity: The Mother of Invention

Highly urbanized areas have been the main drivers of vertical farming's growth. Cities have the density of population and the architectural infrastructure necessary for vertical farms to thrive. They also suffer the most from limitations of distance and scarcity of fertile land.

For city-dwellers, putting a farm in a skyscraper seems like a logical solution to the challenge of sourcing fresh, local produce. Instead of trucking in food from rural areas - a practice that contributes to carbon emissions and often compromises freshness - cities can, in theory, grow their own fruits, vegetables, and greens, and do so sustainably.

6.4. The Crop Stars

Not all crops are suited for vertical farming, though. Leafy greens and herbs are the stars of the show, relishing in the precisely controlled conditions. Other vegetables, like tomatoes, beans, and peppers are grown in limited levels due to their higher resource needs. Staple crops like grains, which require a lot of space, and root crops, which require a lot of depth, are mostly incompatible. However, with continuous advancements and experiments, we can expect to see a wider variety in the future.

6.5. Case Studies of Leading Vertical Farms

Let's take a look at some of today's leading vertical farms.

AeroFarms, based in Newark, New Jersey, is one of the biggest vertical farming companies in the world. Their largest farm, located in a former steel mill, is capable of producing up to two million pounds of food per year.

Singapore's Sky Greens is the world's first commercial vertical farm. They use a rotating "A-Go-Gro" system, where plants rotate for equal exposure to sunlight, thus saving energy costs of artificial lighting.

Bowery Farming, a New York-based startup, uses machine learning to track and analyze over 200 aspects of a plant's life cycle in order to optimize growth conditions.

6.6. The Future: Setting the Stage for Expansion

Although still in its infancy and facing many challenges, the future of vertical farming holds enormous promise. The benefits of being able to grow food in urban areas, close to consumers, and in ways that use fewer resources and offer higher yields are hard to ignore.

As we face increasing pressure to feed a growing global population amid the looming threats of climate change, vertical farming offers a beacon of hope. It's a way to safeguard our food security while also contributing to sustainable urban development.

6.7. Conclusion

From the genesis of vertical farming, through building urban skyscrapers into functional farms, to exploring case studies and looking into the future of this industry, we have uncovered the fascinating journey of vertical farming. It's more than just a new way to grow food—it's also a revolutionary approach to sustainable agriculture. And in our rapidly urbanizing world, it promises an exciting blend of technology, innovation, food security, and greener cities.

Despite the challenges that still need to be addressed, vertical farming is here to stay. The seeds have been sown, and the harvest promises to be bountiful. So, the next time you look at a city skyscraper, you might just be looking at the future of farming.

Chapter 7. From Backyards to Rooftops: Navigating Urban Farming Regulations

Worldwide, urban dwellers have been creatively repurposing their living spaces into lush, productive patches of green, employing everything from traditional soil-based methods to advanced hydroponic systems. This transition from merely decorative to actively productive, though inspiring, meets its fair share of challenges – most significantly, navigating regulations.

As we delve deeper into the intricacies of urban farming, we'll look closely at two prime locations for this horticultural revolution – backyards and rooftops.

7.1. Backyard Farming: Opportunities and Limits

Among the many pockets of potential greenery in an urban landscape, backyards offer a significant level of charm and accessibility. These plots, whether the miniature gardens attached to townhouses or the more substantial spaces behind suburban dwellings, can deliver a significant harvest while adding a touch of beauty to everyday lives.

From constructing raised beds to encouraging community participation, backyard farming champions share stories of success, navigating regulations and overcoming obstacles. As we would learn from the narrative of Mr. Johnson, a retired educator who turned his suburban lawn into a thriving source of beans, peppers, and satisfaction, backyard farming is as intricate as it's fulfilling.

However, not every plant can be grown in every backyard, and not every backyard can be transformed into a farm. Urban agriculture enthusiasts often grapple with zoning ordinances, noise restrictions, and specific restrictions on the type of crops allowed.

For example, depending on regional and local laws, the cultivation of certain vegetables may be prohibited based on concerns about weed control, aesthetics, and even odor. The nature and extent of these restrictions vary dramatically, underscoring the need for the would-be urban agriculturist to diligently research and comply with applicable regulations.

7.2. Rooftop Farming: The Last Frontier

Rooftops, offering an escape from the hustle and bustle beneath, hold immense potential for urban farming. The stories of initiatives like Brooklyn Grange in New York, one of the world's largest rooftop farms, demonstrate how rooftops can harness underused urban resources to produce fresh, local, and sustainable food.

However, transforming a rooftop into a functional farm is fraught with obstacles and regulations, starting with the fundamental issue of whether the roof can support additional weight. This necessitates input from architects, structural engineers, and often local government officials, not to mention potential limitations on altering leased properties.

Building codes frequently impose limitations on the type and extent of alterations that may be made to rooftops, including the installation of green roofs and hydroponic systems. Additionally, health and safety codes may restrict the types of crops that can be grown, particularly when edible plants are involved.

Safe access, too, is of paramount importance when navigating rooftop farming regulations. Some jurisdictions require full stairway access (instead of a simple ladder) for rooftops that host farming activity, and virtually all have strict regulations about safety railings. Lastly, navigating potential legal pitfalls relating to leased properties, insurance, and impact on neighbors must be wisely executed for rooftop farming to take root.

7.3. Understanding Zoning Laws

Many restrictions on urban farming stem from zoning laws, which are designed to separate different types of land uses to prevent conflicts. These laws can limit the size and location of urban farms, the types of crops that can be grown, and even the use of farm animals.

Often, municipal or county planning departments have jurisdiction over these laws. Some cities have begun to update their zoning codes to accommodate urban agriculture, recognizing the social, health, and environmental benefits it can provide. However, in many areas, the process of changing these laws is slow, and existing regulations may discourage or prohibit many types of urban farming activities.

Understanding your local zoning laws and how they impact urban farming activities is a crucial first step towards becoming an urban farmer. Assistance from legal, planning, or agricultural professionals can be invaluable in navigating these complex regulations.

7.4. Dealing with Infrastructure Challenges

The transformation of existing urban infrastructure into farming space, be it backyards or rooftops, does not come without challenges. Critical considerations include water access, soil health, safe and legal disposal of waste, and the prevention of pest and disease issues.

The potential environmental impact of urban farming practices must also be carefully considered, from the risk of contaminated soils in older urban areas to potential runoff of nutrients and pollutants into urban stormwater systems. Regulations governing these areas, from environmental to health codes, must be carefully complied with to ensure urban farming that is safe, sustainable, and legal.

7.5. From Barriers to Green Bridges

Whether in the backyard or on the roof, navigating urban farming regulations is no small task. Every space offers its own challenges and rewards, underpinned by complex local rules and regulations. However, with careful research, awareness of local regulations, and creativity in facing challenges, cultivating city spaces into lush, productive gardens is both possible and rewarding.

So take courage, green-thumbed warriors. Despite the barriers, urban farming represents a transformative opportunity to make our cities greener and our lives healthier. One seed at a time, let's bridge the divide between the urban and the agricultural... from backyards to rooftops, let's nurture this growing revolution. After all, a city fed by its gardens is a city rooted in resilience.

Chapter 8. Community Gardens: Planting the Seed for Social Transformation

The contemporary landscape of urban life, awash with high-rises and honking vehicles, paints a picture of a frantic populace distanced from the quiet charm of pastoral life. Yet, embedded within this bustling milieu, aspirations of a greener future germinate, gradually taking root within urban societies across the globe.

8.1. Seeds of change

The dense urban fabric, characterized by its dearth of open spaces and seemingly at odds with the rural essence of agriculture, has proven a surprisingly fertile ground for the emergence of a new-age farming culture. The concept of community gardens, initially introduced as a means to combat the growing concern surrounding food security and lack of green spaces, has bloomed into a potent catalyst for social transformation.

Growing more than just crops, these gardens have become the groundwork for community-building, socio-economic betterment, and improved environmental sustainability. They span from intricately terraced plots winding down townhouses, to rooftop spreads overlooking city landscapes, to some cleverly designed vertical gardens clinging to steel and glass exteriors of trendy office buildings, seeding an unlikely camaraderie between concrete and green.

8.2. Community building

Community gardens are often the outcome of concerted efforts of devoted residents looking to reshape their neighborhoods. By involving community members in the establishment and maintenance of these green plots, they foster a shared sense of ownership and responsibility. A sown seed becomes an emblem of cooperation, respect, and mutual understanding among diverse community members. The shared act of tending to a common green space instills a potent sense of belonging, of being integral parts of a larger, nature-infused collective.

By providing a common platform, these gardens also become grounds for fostering relationships among different age groups and socio-economic statuses. They bridge generational gaps and bring together varied professions, encouraging knowledge exchanges that extend beyond the realm of gardening.

8.3. Nurturing health and wellness

Just as they nurture plants, community gardens cultivate healthier communities. Engaging in gardening activities has been regularly associated with improved physical and mental wellbeing for participants. Regular tending of plants allows for moderate physical activities, aiding in the maintenance of heart health and body weight.

The potential mental health benefits are arguably on par, if not outweighing the physical. Tranquil gardening activities help reduce stress, anxiety, and depression, providing urban dwellers respite from their frenzied routines. The fresh produce these gardens yield provides access to nutritious food and encourages healthier diets among urban residents, further contributing to their overarching welfare benefits.

8.4. Urban regeneration and environmental implications

Community gardens significantly contribute to urban regeneration, converting neglected and abused land into thriving green spaces. They can turn derelict pieces of land into valuable community assets, imbibing dilapidated zones with new life and a renewed sense of purpose.

On the environmental frontier, these urban oases play a crucial role in improving the overall urban biodiversities - attracting pollinators, birds, and beneficial insects. They promote the absorption of carbon dioxide and release of oxygen, enhance stormwater management, and reduce the urban heat island effect, thereby making cities more resilient to adverse weather effects of climate change.

8.5. Addressing food security

In a world grappling with the growing challenge of food scarcity, community gardens offer a sustainable solution. They facilitate local food production, increasing urban self-sufficiency and reducing dependence on transportation of food from rural farmlands. This not only ensures access to fresh produce but also reduces carbon emissions associated with food transportation.

8.6. The Journey Ahead

The movement towards urban agriculture is just beginning to flower, with community gardens serving as the thriving heart. Municipal and non-governmental policy support can further nurture this grassroots initiative, providing opportunities for more sustainable urban living.

While the road ahead is fraught with difficulty, compounded by urban density, land prices and issues of access, the rewards are too great to ignore. As urban dwellers increasingly embrace the reality of their environmental impact, community gardens offer a beacon of hope in a sometimes impersonal concrete landscape.

Whether it's sharing a freshly picked tomato with a neighbor or working together to compost household waste, every effort plants a seed of change, refining our concept of community and restoring our relationship with the land. These gardens are proving, one plot at a time, that the phrase 'concrete jungle' can have a whole different, and much greener, meaning.

Chapter 9. The Urban Farming Revolution: Impact on Food Security

Our planet has been in the throes of rapid urbanization. The United Nations reports that 68% of the world population is likely to be living in urban areas by 2050. With this shift, our cities are becoming denser, and green spaces are disappearing rapidly, replaced by concrete structures.

Despite the unyielding advance of concrete and steel, a green revolution is taking root. All over the world, individuals, communities, and organizations recognize the urgency to fight against this urban sprawl and create spaces for growth. But this isn't about mere aesthetics, nor is it purely about environmental conservation. This revolution represents a struggle for one of the most basic human needs: food security.

9.1. The Chronicles of Urban Farming

Food security, as defined by the United Nations' Committee on World Food Security, is "the condition in which all people, at all times, have physical and economic access to sufficient, safe and nutritious food that meets their dietary needs and food preferences for an active and healthy life."

To put it simply, urban agriculture is about growing food in the city—for the city. Bringing food production closer to where the majority of people live offers us a unique solution to many of the modern world's problems, from food insecurity to environmental sustainability.

Urban farming also has the advantage of drastically reducing the distance food travels from farm to table, transforming food deserts into thriving communities, fostering local economies, and connecting urban dwellers to the process of cultivating the food they eat.

9.2. Feeding Cities: An Underground Movement

In the face of increasing urbanization and a strained global food system, urban farmers have taken ingenuity to new levels. From transforming derelict buildings into vertical farms to integrating aquaponics systems into city architecture, urban agriculture is a testament to human creativity in the face of adversity.

These grassroots initiatives are adapting to the urban landscape, utilizing rooftops, vacant lots, balconies, and even forgotten railway arches to cultivate a variety of crops. Growing practices are as varied as the urban farmers themselves. While some use hydroponics—growing plants in a nutrient-rich solution instead of soil—to maximize space and productivity, others rely on traditional soil-based methods and introduce beneficial insects for pest control.

Vertical farms are particularly interesting. The concept takes the traditional farming method of planting single-level crops and flips it - literally - on its side. By planting crops on vertically stacked levels, these farms can provide fresh produce to urban residents while occupying minimal ground space.

9.3. Nurturing Communities: The Social Impact

Urban agriculture is not solely about growing fresh local food. It's about reinstating communities. These green spaces often serve as community hubs, offering residents a place to connect, learn, and contribute to their neighborhood. It gives a whole new meaning to "grassroots organizations."

Through these community gardens, individuals who would typically be uninvolved in the food production process can explore growing food, learning about nutrition, and share homegrown produce with their families and neighbors. They also provide employment, offering a feasible means of income for people who may struggle with traditional work environments.

9.4. From Greener Cities to Resilient Nations

Investments in urban agriculture can pave the way for cities to be more sustainable and resilient in the face of crisis and change. Not only does it increase food security and access to fresh produce, but these urban gardens also enhance a city's resilience to climate change by reducing urban heat and providing habitat for local wildlife.

However, for the full potential of urban farming to be realized, it requires support—not merely tolerance—from policy-makers, architects, and the general public for the dedication and resolve of urban farmers. It requires open dialogue, policy revision, publicity, and educational programming to address the multifaceted challenges of urban farming—and then we may begin to see the transformation of our cityscapes.

Urban farming offers us a tantalizing taste of our possible future—one where cities are not just providers of jobs, but also hubs of green, sustainable living. With every sunrise illuminating the green terrains amidst the concrete jungle, we are reminded of a simple truth—that nature and humans can co-exist, not just survive but thrive, together in an era of change and challenges.

The Urban Farming Revolution is just beginning, and its potential is limited only by our collective ingenuity, commitment, and willingness to re-imagine the future. It's a silent but urgent battle—not for dominance, but for symbiosis—a battle that we cannot afford to lose.

Where streets were once cold and grey, there now grow tomatoes, kale, and pungent herbs. Each seed planted in the heart of our cities is a revolutionary act, a declaration of independence from a broken food system. And as we make room for more seeds, we're making room for a more resilient future.

So let's take up our shovels, let's get our hands dirty and join the ranks. This is The Urban Farming Revolution.

Chapter 10. Paving the Way: Policy Innovations for Urban Farming

Urban agriculture is not a new concept, but its resurgence in the 21st century has brought unique challenges. As we navigate this unfamiliar terrain, we find ourselves confronted with a concrete labyrinth of zoning laws, regulations, and lack of support structures developed with traditional agriculture in mind. This journey will give us a close look at the ways our urban farming pioneers are pushing past these barriers and making significant changes.

10.1. Navigating the Zoning Maze

One of the primary obstacles urban farmers face is zoning. Zoning regulations were established with the needs of sprawling rural farms in mind, not compact urban plots. For many city farmers, this predicament has meant fighting tooth and nail for the right to farm in their own backyards or vacant lots, facing restrictions on raising livestock and even sometimes plants.

Innovative policy changes have begun sprouting in several cities. Toronto, for instance, introduced a zoning amendment in 2013 allowing for urban agriculture in all zones of the city. In Detroit, a city experiencing a significant revival of urban farming, activist Malik Yakini took the zoning bull by the horns. Frustrated by the restrictions, he and a group of passionate urban farmers crafted the pioneering Detroit Urban Agriculture Ordinance, proposed in 2013. This landmark legislation, though not yet passed, has spurred a citywide conversation on the benefits and possibilities of urban farming.

10.2. Building Urban Agriculture Support Structures

Without any existing support systems, prospective urban farmers often shoulder all the burdens and risks without access to important resources. This bottleneck has the potential to hinder the journey for even the most committed individuals.

In response, various cities have started looking at agriculture extension services to provide resources, training, and advice to urban farmers. For example, Seattle's urban farming program offers soil testing, composting classes, and crop planning assistance, all tailored to small-scale, urban contexts. Moreover, organizations like Chicago's Advocates for Urban Agriculture work tirelessly to provide education and space for community discussions regarding urban farming policies.

10.3. Rewriting the Food Safety Rules

A crucial policy concern for urban farming is food safety. Traditional agriculture has relied heavily on chemical pesticides and fertilizers, substances that are often ill-suited for urban environments. Similarly, animal farming in urban settings necessitates policies on animal welfare and control of disease risk.

Several cities are making strides with these issues. Philadelphia's Soil Kitchen event, organized with the help of the EPA, provides free soil testing to detect heavy metals or other contaminants, ensuring safe growing spaces throughout the city. San Francisco, on the other hand, has implemented a groundbreaking ordinance that not only allows but encourages community members to grow and sell locally produced foods, while defining clear guidelines for maintaining safety standards.

10.4. Fostering a Local Economy

As urban farms become more common, there has been a growing need to integrate these operations into the local economy. This includes new policies for selling farm products, tax incentives for urban farming, and even farm-to-school programs.

New York City is leading the way with legislation allowing urban farmers to sell their products directly to consumers through farm stands and farmers markets. By removing obstacles for direct selling, this policy encourages community engagement and sustains local food systems. Moreover, in Baltimore, a property tax credit for urban farms was established in 2019, easing the financial strain for farmers and incentivizing more urban agriculture.

Urban agriculture has the potential to revolutionize our cities, transforming them into sustainable, green hubs teeming with local food production. The aforementioned policy innovations are just the beginning. As we create an inclusive urban agricultural policy, we will have the capacity to bolster local economies, improve food security, and nourish our communities from within. The fight may be tough, but the fruits of this labor can redefine what it means to be urban. The 'Battle of the Beets' is not just about growing plants in a concrete environment; it's about nurturing a greener future.

Chapter 11. The Future Harvest: Visions of Tomorrow's Urban Farms

As the dawn of a new day breaks, urban farmers are already at work, meeting the food needs of city dwellers. Today's urban farms are courtyards converted into kitchen gardens, roofs cultivated into nurturers of fresh produce, and terraces turned into miniature food forests, but what will the urban farms of tomorrow look like?

11.1. Envisioning Urban Farms

If current global trends are any indication, urban farms of the future will be brimming with technologically advanced systems and eco-friendly solutions for sustained food production. Advances in automated agriculture and plant biology will usher in a new era of urban farming, characterized by smart hydroponics facilities, vertical farms, and floating greenhouses.

Though many of these advancements may seem like science fiction, they're closer to becoming reality than ever before. For example, vertical farming, which maximizes the use of limited space by cultivating crops in vertically stacked layers, is steadily gaining traction in cities worldwide. Future urban farms may see multi-level structures dedicated to growing a variety of crops year-round, irrespective of weather fluctuations, pest infestations, or soil fertility issues.

Floating greenhouses, another innovative concept, take advantage of aquatic spaces for farming. These facilities use solar energy to power operations and recirculate water, greatly reducing fresh water and energy use. Imagine clusters of these floating farms lining our urban waterfronts producing vast quantities of food, energy, and even clean water.

11.2. Advanced Technologies in Urban Farming

The integration of technology into urban farming systems is already a reality. Hydroponic systems, drip irrigation, and farm management software have greatly improved efficiency and productivity. Tomorrow's farms could see even more sophisticated tech, such as AI-driven machines for seeding, weeding, watering, and harvesting, reducing the need for human labor and making urban agriculture a more viable livelihood.

Alongside automation, the use of data and analytics will transform future urban farming. Satellite imagery, climate data, and sensors will help farmers maximize output and minimize waste. Connected devices will alert farmers when a plant needs water or fertilizer, ensuring optimum growth conditions and reducing the overuse of resources. This predictive farming will not only enable urban farmers to anticipate crop yields but also mitigate risks and adverse effects of unexpected climate conditions.

11.3. Sustainable Practices in Future Urban Farms

Making urban farming sustainable will be a critical aspect of building the cities of the future. Future farms will incorporate closed-loop systems, where waste becomes a resource. For instance, organic waste from restaurants could feed composting systems, producing nutrient-rich fertilizer, while livestock waste could be converted into biogas for heat and electricity.

Aquaponics, a system that combines fish farming and hydroponics, is another sustainable urban agriculture model. The waste produced by fish serves as organic food for plants, and the plants naturally filter the water for fish. Future urban farms may feature aquaponic systems installed on rooftops or in basements, offering city dwellers a source of fresh local produce and seafood.

11.4. Community Integration and Urban Farming

Urban farms of the future will not only be places where food is grown but also centers of community engagement and education. Farm-to-table experiences, farm-related workshops, and apprenticeships can bring city dwellers closer to their food sources and foster deeper connections among community members.

Furthermore, urban farms could help to mitigate numerous social issues in populated areas. By offering job opportunities and green spaces, they could contribute to crime reduction, social inclusion, and improved mental health, making cities not only more sustainable but also more livable.

11.5. Changing the Urban Landscape

In a world where more people are expected to live in cities, the question is not whether urban farming will be part of our future, but rather, how cities and their inhabitants will adapt to and integrate these systems. Experts predict that cities of the future will be green and filled with lush landscapes housing bountiful gardens, floating greenhouses, and multi-storey vertical farms.

While it's a challenging feat, the transformation of current cityscapes into vibrant, food-producing spaces represents a momentous shift in the way we view cities. Today's stark, concrete skylines may soon be speckled with pockets of green, revealing a stunning blend of urban and rural that's both functional and appealing from an aesthetic perspective.

The Battle of the Beets continues and the future of urban farming holds promise. The marrying of advanced technologies, sustainable practices, community integration, and reimagined landscapes may together reshape urban food production, signalling hope for a resilient, green future.